NIAGARA & GOVERNMENT

Also by Phil Hall

Conjugation
Guthrie Clothing: The Poetry of Phil Hall
Notes from Gethsemani
The Small Nouns Crying Faith
Killdeer
The Little Seamstress
White Porcupine
An Oak Hunch
Trouble Sleeping
Hearthedral: A Folk-Hermetic
The Unsaid
Amanuensis
Old Enemy Juice
Why I Haven't Written
A Minor Operation
Homes
Eighteen Poems

NIAGARA & GOVERNMENT
Phil Hall

PEDLAR PRESS | ST. JOHN'S

Copyright © Phil Hall 2020

Pedlar Press supports copyright. Copyright fuels creativity, encourages diverse voices, promotes free speech, and creates a vibrant culture. Thank you for buying an authorized edition of this book and for complying with copyright laws by not reproducing, scanning, or distributing any part of it in any form without permission.
You are supporting writers and allowing Pedlar to continue to publish books for every reader.

All Rights Reserved
For information, write Pedlar Press at
113 Bond Street, St John's NL A1C 1T6 Canada

COVER ART	Phil Hall
DESIGN	Mark Byk
TYPEFACES	Calluna and Calluna Sans

Printed in Canada at Coach House Printing, Toronto ON

LIBRARY AND ARCHIVES CANADA CATALOGUING IN PUBLICATION
Niagara & Government / Phil Hall.
Hall, Phil, 1953– author.

Poems.
Canadiana 2020021179X | ISBN 978-19-89424-03-2 (softcover)

I. TITLE.

LCC PS8565.A449 N53 2020 | DDC C811/.54—dc23
First Edition

ACKNOWLEDGEMENTS
The publisher wishes to thank the Canada Council for the Arts and the NL Publishers Assistance Program for their generous support of our publishing program.

tatibitexto
pulsional

I

Typo

It could be a typo   good on you for catching that

all is ruined & I am a failure   or it could be the only escape from this waiting room   at this dump

•

Barn flight shadows   above swollen   Carbon Creek

a liver-spotted   finger-word   *inwit*   rushes by   wig off

no distances   the sward   become skin   the *sweard*   (OE)

almost   still   here is the Body   rack-less   before *click*   the machine

Gutenberg   & Henry Ford   have kept us apart   far too long

•

The poorer the roof   *the more Os on it*

I cherish   not clarity   no   our demotic scrawl

Translation

At first   leaving Latin   we took the Latin Rd   west

all of the landmarks   were familiar   zebras under bridges
solariums   gurgling cores   roundabouts

by noon   Greenwich   had begun to offer   storied gardens
Forsooth in bloom   Spilled Milk Lungwort

a snake   had to keep near   a wishing-well

purple Indeedium   covert dovecotes   elevated rest-stops

by evening   a coast through   mangled savannahs
toward Kingfisher's Pt

on the radio   Ornette Coleman's *Soapsuds*   Charlie Haden bass

next morning   heading out   saw oxcarts abandoned
waved to local circuses

dabblers   on their knees   in the fields
shouted out to us   in a tongue half Tenure   half Congo

we roll in late   on fumes   to Howl Town
note   *Everyone at Fair Grounds*

the World Saxophone Orchestra   on stage   playing "Selim Sivad"
we were sucked toward David Murray's scribble

pit-lights   running off generators   shone harsh   alternative girders
through the gallimaufry   the farrago

we blended in   started dancing

The Lyric

In Memoriam Tomas Tranströmer (1931-2015)

This body   a circular arrow   loosed   spinning   inside a flagstone

ah   as in Hans Arp   an ankle   fits an instep

the high plateaus   unlost   I say unlost   though it's not true

a whistle   of sea lily   powder   in a flying shard   of limestone

ah   as in Hans Arp   an ankle   fits an instep

the sleeping positions   endless

•

Acting crazy
we were stopped
             by a stand-up bass
on its side in the pasture

morning   no one else around

the angel who grew inside it   like a snail
has abandoned it   & gravity

cello   viola   lute
each housed a different breed of angel

Don't say   angel   that's stupid

in its burning curiosity
about E#
       each   *as if*
was willing to volute   wear   & pull   a shell

each drew   its own   inexplicable
now common   dank   trail

Run & find strings

·

To tell what happened to you   is not a poem

there is not enough in the story of your life to make poetry

 yet roars   *The Lyric*
a calamitous wall   by the platform   you wait on

 little black freight train   match-sticks   & epoxy
each car full of _____

 start your silly lists

archaisms   desperate gerunds   *faux picante*

·

The day Grandmother died
a parcel came for her   no return address

 a photo album   with an elk embossed on the cover

snap-shots
         she was accidentally in
throughout her simple life
              She happened
 to be walking by

& two sketches of her
 done in secret by strangers

each wayward image   culled
 from other peoples' photo albums
rummage sales   landfill

 a wide hat & a scarf along a ship's rail

thumb-blur   a puffy sleeve   60s glasses

 protest marches   wedding deceptions

kids held high   a little bare foot so like an ear   Rare Beach

 security   a mirror flash   then lab scans

Tell us the story of each photo

I don't have time   I can't recollect

then she said   laughing   coughing
 Arms wide   rush   to meet the parade

we buried her album with her
 so no you can't see it

Arms wide   I try to   Gran

 like a   like a

             •

 Now I too   get to hear the cicada   & say so

its no-carapace blues   pierce mine

 the phrase   *all the time in the world*   is a pencil sharpener

to squeeze the I'm   out of a word   don't squeeze

 are you carrying fervour   or currying favour

the line   with no hook   is my fish

Fireworks

  Rhythm   not light   spells
parts of a story   buried   a long time

half-close your eyes   & squint   as you crowd in

hear the steady   pace   of the launched whistles

       ·

A price per rocket   has set this beat   this order

paraded thumping   fizzlers   duds

one flag-apparition   then a speed-up   to finale

panic   a rush-to-seed   *flim-flam*

       ·

Blooms spike   the blood fast   now to show
how raunchy   how reckless   money is

       ·

Shot-at   (un-shot-at)   the Dark   is darker
it whups nearer   Silence

too   has darkened   deepened

for a moment   the date   is 18-something

sulfur smoke   adrift   in stump fields
bogs   wagon-scarred   *dour*

Hitler Spring

after Montale

In Charlottesville   piqued rapturous   white faces
thrown into the air   in triumph

settle back   rabid-sure   at the curb   again

toy bobble-heads   in jailed shops   nod & grimace
as a TV-realtor   campaigns by   declaiming Democracy's buy-out

surveil-ertained   harmless & silly   no one is blameless

a fog in each deposed hand   condones forgetting

while in packed stadiums   giant pigs   eat giant sunflowers
to cheers of   *Crotch & Hate*

out of mines full of garbage   a sour mob-hiss

yet in gnarled Greece   along shaded   moist   vineyard rows
transparent   sea-coloured   rundles   & verticils

have never spelled   *pandemonium*   past the first three letters

& on a low roof   in Poughkeepsie NY
like the mighty   gospel-diva   Mavis Staples   testifying

a commotion sunflower   rises   & turns
its wide eye   a tight no of seeds

The Leap

My back experiences the world
a world   I guess   in its way

but would not recognize me

we have never faced each other
 we go our own ways

I deny my father   I deny my son

I forget I have a back

     ·

 Severely backward
or a ruined husk   wheezing

with no eyes or ears   no smell
or taste   no patience or aim

my back knows only a touch
near to breaking

from kindness it turns away

     ·

Wake up   my creature

masticulate   yr dirty ballads   yr call to worms   yr hump-ditties

let fly   yr gut-anguish

snarl yr   eeny-meeny   why-me / why-not-me   song   now

before thinking twice   forecloses

·

Blood means nothing
family almost killed me

I say *gek*   to progress   in theory

l'art des fous   I would emulate

I even read books backwards   left-handed
flipping   glossary to epigraph

daidala to pageantry

·

But when I jump   I never jump backwards

even if I've had it   with everything
I always jump face-first

I want out   but I want in

that spit & paste   wing-device   from Knossos
its pinions floundering   into the rot-gut sea

·

"the whole thrust of Western civilization"
still has my trust   yep   that's me   fully clothed

at Lascaux   so I have to kill myself

I have to plunge   behind error's exhibits
I have to set on fire   my 2 vol   *Life of Sigmund Freud*

thumbed once   desultorily

I have to gnaw   my own slick knob-joint

·

What falling tastes like is

what *plummetting*   presents as   is

an archive   of everyone's wrong answers

that by accumulative shuffle
 are becoming   right answers   *fast*

but long after it matters

·

I will be buried   or burnt   face up   too   probably
though I land   on each day   face down   face first   a mess

splat   *grrrr*   *& polyphony*

·

A garbled failure   I get up   & say   *I'm fine*

up I get   & make the poem   say it's fine

Fabergé & Pelt

I hate this poem   look how the ego
in a snoot of syntax

grows another tail from its o
to make a second g   & thus write   egg

& not just   egg   but *egg*   italics as class
an old queen of an   *egg*

never to be eaten   by the masses
but worshipped   by those $ in the know

•

I didn't find my Voice   didn't study for it   don't wield one

wovms thwo vdhie thw zpf jl f3fkd ei f;a ek a;bv , qo je fo ahroe

instead   I found my Township   indifference   trampled   to a slur
it is named after a Lieutenant Governor's wife's lapdog   1 of 3

thei aw 5js gh49s ;a vf te f;af eifs stgsk f; UE SCMD KS TUA kf eg

there are maple Huron skull fragments & sea spines in my lingo
I put up the No Trespassing signs myself   & am my own poacher

p frehi v,. cx,x jfkl eqf e foxc e jl xo fj leia flf ri la ejls 'ao cl a'

this is Silence's legendary   stretched pelt   *hit*   so as to be worn

The Snowman

Today   the hard *i*   in *white*   seems garish

too perky   especially for snow   or Greek walls

what   would be a better word for   *white*

a deep-track   rag-leaf   *what*   I am of

        ·

Not interrogatory   a rounder   rangier   throat-step

scrolled   unacceptance   greying   deepens

& the glare   of those walls   on Skyros   or Crete   fades

its own pan-religion   this flaked   duller   lime-wash

        ·

A crossless   defeated / undefeated   *what*

I cannot   blindly   lean back against   of an evening

but frozen   must stand   where what I am   falls on what I am

gladly   a stone of coal   or shard of bark   for witness

        ·

My warily   hummed   *uh*   one tug less   exact

while basted   fabled   destinations   glow   hot white

& squeeze   omega   to a spike   of mastery

a painter's trick   a laughter-dot   in an eye

Past Once

If my mouth is stuffed with stories
I cannot be suckled by the moment

    •

Have I ever heard   a no-story   sound

~~once~~   ~~between towns~~   ~~at night~~
~~standing still~~   ~~& alone~~   ~~in a stony field~~

    •

A ripple   of wet   suctioning   smacks

~~the rocks were nursing on silence~~

~~the rocks were nursing silence~~

    •

Dark humps   cupping   *& un-cupping*
an unspoken   shut up

II

Local Produce

If it is understandable   it is not   true to life

a survey   over-grown   misplaces   the back 40

the illegitimacy   of starting poor   in the enisled counties

squats in   & aims   to ground   every flourish

to gather   patches   *toward*   a landscape   then

the way Cezanne did   or Celan did   in gobbets   & touch-ups

quilt-frames   *teeming creels*   *auctions*   *& rummage*

time to sit in the woods   or get off the poet

Typo-mundus begins at the joiner's T-square

goddamn Wordsworth but hooray crop circles

to put a frame on the land is to slip a halter metaphor

over the muzzle of a wild stallion the woods

is to prod a corncob bit between its square teeth

a simile is to hag-ride all that is Other

even if the horse Dobbin Night isn't so wild

a nag it has been ridden bareback many times

all the radiant huge light first growth pine

is long gone failed farms almost made a go of it

on top of failed farms *Schliemann found* *Troy layered*

Al Purdy mutters & sighs loudly not really

long gone into newsprint kindling antiques matches

what keeps *our meditation* *from going deeper*

metaphor (the dead horse) & the reference to Troy

Local boys   their names on cenotaphs   *Hall Thurston*

Thoon   Imbrios   Phylakos   Private Leg   Private Ball

or   at The Front   1916   the rearranged   risqué   collagists

their helmets   empty   spouting   pin-holes   of mud-light   pluck

image   a bag of arms   *image*   a bag of heads   singing   *Ubu*

cut   back home   1923   Royal Medical Students   U of T   McGill

reading dull   Robert Frost   while inheriting the landscape   X 7

weekend hikes   eugenics   field boards   Massey-Harris

whose woods these are   Algoma reds   humorous cadavers

to dab   rapids-white   pronounce over   legend-harvest   tag

of Hector   & Lysander   & such great names   as these   but

Hall Thurston   is no one   really   important   my stupid   rubber devil

my joke heteronym   *what*   half-brother   hunger   my class rage

stinkweed   milkweed   the lost son   ragweed   fire weed

my Dollar Store   alphabet stencil   poor mouth   half a door knob

Hall Thurston   only he opens   the access-route   to the swamp

Oh don't say   *swamp*   say   *marsh*   young man   that's nicer

& don't   you dare   say   *what*   to me   say   *pardon*

say   *thank you*   *for the cenotaph*   kind Sirs

.

I don't know   how misspelled   my people were

or where   they landed   first here   or why

their skills pissed away   their finger-ends kept   in matchboxes

bitterness clung to   a porch of   crushed smoke

splayed   flat-orange   birch   fardels

gouached   root-cellars   *caking*   dank cisterns

their abandoned churches   holes in the ground

or doubling   as hen houses   *can't think myself here*

lime-smutch   wainscot   pew   ovum   now

weekenders   from TO   dig in homestead   dumps

for blue   medicine bottles   & green   gin bottles

that were   the balm   & the ruin   of caring

the balm   & the ruin   of caring   hi-ho

sucky caring   & memory   spited

complexity   dumbed-down   to pap   & drivel

post cards   & greeting cards   details blacked out

from the blowsy   clearance   highlands   of Scotland

to the aggregate   Tory   highlands   of Lanark County

I want my wee can   I want my wee can   or

never darken   my doorway   again   you bastard

& they never did   & that was the end of it

& the stupid can was never found

 faerie   & pike   islands   disowned

for a frozen log-chain   & the chewed stem of a pipe

In place   of the old   first places

& out   of a darkened   doorway   comes

again   *not again!*   high-minded   Art   mitered

swinging   its own   scented   pap   & drivel

Heritage & Culture   fossils   *dialectical primitive*   et al

& all   that keeps   invasion   or the plague

from swamping   every system   we rely on   it seems

is this frame   set over   this tamed   scrape

a realistic painting   its cult of a date   by a name

its crippling   comfort   its own   petting-zoo   title

The Road   to the Beaver   Marsh

when metaphor   stops   soothing us   numb

the frangible   destitute   intricacies   begin

if there weren't archives   & parades   in the way

we would have   more sense evidence   than ballyhoo

headline   we are self-destructing   others

headline   cornucopia = coelacanth

the hunt the climb   the wag the pillory   the feast

the hunt the climb the wag   the pillory the feast

Can't see the fly when holding the swatter

animals & vegetables are minerals too

when will they give an honorary doctorate to Anonymous

I'm not so good   in the woods   anymore

I need a hippy replacement

what blocks revelation   the pun

easy fun   is how we stop   short of   transformation

the lyric   is only interested   in itself

no poem   takes priority   over safety

how to plod   enough   to change   into

any artifact   or entity   *die*   join the mish-mash

look how   the long poem   dies   & doesn't die

happy   to muck about   allow   & accumulate

happy   to get so wrong   this blustering flit

I have trampled on   my new white   notebook

bent   muddied   & torn   its pages

now the prison guard   biker chicks   are pulling in

one leans out   from her greasy   saddle   to knock

my Stetson off   while others crouch   to pet

a wounded   rat snake   in the warm gravel

where is   that folk song   I promised them   eh

a silly ballad   ticky-tacky   about local   produce

here it is   My Sweet Ones   here it is

between worth   & commodity   this shaky juju zone

hydro with a carapace

goldfinches over the septic

III

Stan Dragland's *Wall*

The Age of Wood
still has an extant   if battered   larynx

its survey map   molders   in our carpal tunnels
as we grip plastic handles

the larynx   has to be assembled   to be believed in
from scattered detritus   & there is no manual

to find the map   we best journey into the hands
that drew the map

unscrolled   wormy   its drawroads   & timelines
can still be followed

if not by barons   at least by fingers

the event of a thread   Anni Albers

•

The horizontal knob you see   on the vertical brown thing
linking the two turquoise boards

turns   releasing the white board   which slides to the right
across the brown board

revealing the picture

•

Then it is   as if on display
were a church organ   a calliope   *a hurdy-gurdy*

in various partial guises   for all pokers & pullers to explore

this larynx   is a muted voice box   of ply-   & paint
& screw-hole   & toy

this map has tunnels   reeds   soft hammers   foot-pedals
rescue-ropes   gauze   & knockers

the only sounds   the larynx of the Age of Wood
makes now   *whispering*

are from its sliding parts   & hidden doorlettes
yawing   tracting

curiosity   =   friction   =   music

an invisible sawdust rises   & we breathe it   treed

.

Stan Dragland's *Wall*   is also a demonstration-model
of the legendary   Kindling Tongue

pulled down like a school map
it is a zoo of best-guess fragments

from that fabled garden   known as First Growth
harked to   invoked

there   the hand plane   & the bucksaw
are snail-shapes   D-shapes

& the circle   *n'est pas*   le wheel

we may think we hear in it   birch bark canoes
log cabins   plank sidewalks   footbridges

a box of matchsticks   a rocker
clothes pegs   & books being read

but these have   here   retreated again
to before function

& are once more nearly creatures
almost   écriture

unbent   un-named
pre-   the exile of application

pre-   the shame of measurement

Wall   is to the Eden of First Growth
in ruins among us   an altar

Kindling Tongue   beckons
with the shaved curl   of a small   r

·

Behold   the Green Man reviled   hunted
squatting   in back yard tree houses

a filthy swinger   of alley sticks   at cats
his job   *increpation*

the Wode King   & his wife Splinter   besieged
are now salvage

canted along any beach   in the Age of Formaldehyde
the Age of Chipboard

but if you hold   secretly   this peeled staff at night
you may talk

·

The large circle with the handle on it   comes out
& behind it   will be another circle

which is the cover of a well   scrounged from a beach

*the circle   is covered with gold foil
 that comes from the wrap   Simon was given*

*in Tromsø Norway
 after finishing the Midnight Sun Marathon*

·

Our bombed & looted Pedestrian Archives
have been rescued   into a design

this field as gizmo
between us & the blank wall of the gallery

come all ye   who are *drawn to*   any little portico
or flaw in a tapestry

  each Chinese finger trap   each Jacob's ladder
each rusty spigot

by *drawn to flaws*   we have always meant   *to sense*
an elusive aspect of one's fallen self

in the damaged concordance of the earth

Wall   is an invite   unto intricacies
that point back to a reassessment of surfaces

.

Oil painting is an abandonment of theatre   & a scam of depth

even Action Painting is a fossil of movement   frozen dried   past

Pollock's frenzy   poleaxed   flattened   *don't touch*   *pay*

in contrast   this wall's literary parallel-venture   is Ronald Johnson's
   festive avant   *ARK*   built on the model of the Watts Towers

in a devastated & rigorous part of LA   low art to climb

.

Attached to the back of the circle
is a box containing spent shotgun shells

& surrounded by cartoons

.

Colours on canvases
are great white lamniform sharks   *Miró*

 words on pages
are layers & broilers   chickens   *Maeve Binchy*

but chicken-sharks exist

& that rare hybrid   *Miróbinchy*

.

So folk art   & fine art   are one

folk   in its shed materials
fine   in its poetics of   *amodal*   disrepair

as with the first *papier collés*   by Braque 1912
we must bring to this wall   a multiple perspective

a prescient *shrapnel* regard

the war to end all wars   not 1914   is coming
if there are no trees   we can't breathe

in order to see more than dry wit here
or the un-pristine   obsessiveness   of character

we must entertain devastation & gullibility at once
studied bewilderment

to baton   its form-challenge
to ingest its dialectic   its juxta-pose   as text

we must inlay child's play   with history's faith

Chaucer's   *at regard of*   is to   *heed*

.

Abolish the distance between the word & the thing

each board in this wall   is a word
a spell has turned into   a gravity-thingy   a tongue depressor

accept   all at once   *Wall*'s component hunches
to hold articulation down awhile   *nga*   *gna*

that word there   *liquid as woodlands*   says George Oppen
has never touched its thing

this word here   has only ever hung from its thing's toe

.

Elocution has been stopping
the nursery-words & the grub-words

from crawling out
of that secret room in the basement

because we could say *appendectomy*
we could not say *sister*

•

native speech of the obstacle   in this manner is the fable avoided

Claude Royet-Journoud

•

From this angle   the tinker is master
& the hack-work   fine

Wall is Bakhtin's *carnivale   *as Huck's raft

& Cornell's fetish-dioramas   as First Aid kits

Wall is a touch table   free hotdogs in the park
cul-de-sac   whack-ball at dusk   advent calendars

*ensemble   *as abandoned mill

Every machine   contains   a cow path   Kenneth Burke

•

Shucks   I just made a thing   & kept adding to it
scraps from the barn

*no name   call it   *Wall

*my materials were chosen almost at random   *says the tinker

*in the spur of   *says the master
with humility   & deflection

hiding up in   not wearing   the laurel

Marlatt   Kroetsch   Reaney   Nichol   Thibaudeau
Dewdney   Kiyooka

neighbouring near-faiths   assimilated   honoured
 folked

Some of the boards were donated by friends

        ·

Tongue   Staff   Larynx   Zoo   Map

(we pray to)   serve up
 sound   weight   pace   & colour

each quick   *hold-it*   an expectant clapper

 set us near to   a reed   or gut-string
as if playing   Statues

 a new claw   a seventh arm   an h on a knee

as we postulate   boundless inclusion
 through imperfection

instill in us   a gather-trust

 a grab-sing   a vow-try
we hope   we find   we are

        ·

Weathered texture   is *Wall*'s costume

the grin of the leg-pull   is in it as a well

detour-minism   & boney-os

Proximity

If I wake up too early
everything has no vital intent yet

*I've accumulated all this junk
& try to treasure it   because I am afraid
to be blank   hollow   silent*

I do not have   the gumption
of a solo

•

Then I'll move one thing closer to another

or further from it   or try it beside something else

until proximity wakes up
the tourniquet that is association

then objects   & words   freed of mere curiousness
begin to say   *yes*   in relation

& to teach me   how to say   *yes*
in relation   as if well

•

I am curating   strident   toward a fable
of leaky worth

it is not enough

but it does lead me between stagnation
& redemption

it does extrapolate   this unlikely tongue
I am not ashamed of anymore

Bottom

I

Early traffic   on Elm Grove Rd
        the bastion   the bastillion   of its combust

a hummingbird   at the plastic-strawberry feeder
        the burling   hyphen   of its thrum

hay-twine   & a tin-foil   pie-plate

this folk art   whirligig   letters

        ·

Our kettle   screams   & screams

the mirror above it   blears   & fogs

in this greying   dawn kitchen   I clean my glasses

as I head-write   *tea-kettle   tear-kettle*

22 years without a drink   many notebooks
many dazed speakers

not   *Once*   but   *nonce*

our kettle   sings   & sings

2

    I kept going back out   to work on my story

  it was all I had
   its badness   my only orthodoxy

  it wouldn't be publishable when I was finished with it
   a lost Brothers Grimm   horrific pathetic low-down   all true

He was swallowed by a talking fish

 while belting out   to the stars in a puke-puddle
 them old sweet   Rub Alcohol Blues

      ·

 Bottom is a blackhead mistaken for a period
 if I hadn't cleaned myself up I might have died

      ·

 effondrement

 abgrund

 l'eau

3

  Sometimes the only way to show rage too late
for yr Mom or Dad   is to kill yrself with the hooch

same way he killed himself   or she killed herself

so you pick up   that empty bottle   *after bottle*   of theirs
    & tip it to the light   to find a bare wedge   one drop left

then up-end it   on yr tongue   & wait

 for that flaming knot of sloppy melodrama
to fall on you   like a solid case

 like loyalty   or helpless sputtering   or a remembered slap

or no alternative   like a falsie nipple   or a gun of yr very own
    like *why didn't you protect me*   like a white-nosed spleen

or déjà vu   *that lie*   or rage   *that lie*

4

Hummingbird   as a name
is as if to   have no name

is to be   known as   one's own   main act

(as if my name   had been   *Drinkingman*)

·

Hum   for short
or *Drink*   for short

one quick open syllable each

one ope syll

·

Dear Hum

I hove   & point   too / still   out / at
the old urge   to   *fail*

stay in   & run the fan   all day
for the blur   & fuss of it

to do   what I am called   *Fill*

'til I am   loud-known as   *Feel*

'til *am* is   down-thrown   *fall*

·

Easier to play with words

to let language break   as if clever

than to face that song no one has heard

we all sing to ourselves a version of

5

  Pity the table pounders
the last-call shouters & clappers

 singing along   they find themselves   *below* Bottom

they can see where they might have white-knuckled
 their self-pity   to a stop   corked the lies   mid-guzzle

& started a new   dry   ballad   stations ago

 but by now they are tied to the railway tracks
& John Barleycorn is greasing his fake handle-bars

 as the Wabash   that last drop   *roaches-in-the-liver*   screams

      .

 How Porter Wagoner   & George Jones   are singing of the wreck
is an ad campaign   not rebels / not angels   they are pall-bearers

in hillbilly-rhinestone   Nudie suits   not a porch in sight

*blunderingly ostentatious   stage lights   in prime gels
feeding off of   wage corpses   & cannon fodder*

the Grand Ole Opry   is a church   of train-wrecks   who pay

6

Drink

Dear Honey-Water-Sipper

a playing card   & a clothes-peg   march
cack-cack-cack

between the spokes   of my carved   wind-wheel
rough likeness   of your wisp   of a visit

Dear Drum-Hatcher   Dear Flap-Ratchet

I am watching   what I've assembled   spin / clack

Dear Little Ruby Turbine   Dear Feather-Pin

·

Hum

Dear Drink   you   Son Of a Bitch

you may mean well   but stop the histrionics
all that   conjugation

all that naming   & personifying

I am no backyard   for your naiveté   & cleverness

even your spelling   of your   as yr   offends me

your folksiness   in sobriety
has a tag-number   & specimen drawer   smell to it

by wordsmithy   by birdsmithy

you cannot   dry me out of   my song

7

  Those wine bottles   that at base
have a hollow   a bell-shape   you can put a thumb up in

 when I first stopped drinking
I stood as if   inside   under   a glass bell
 surrounded by booze   but dry

all I talked about was drinking
 & not drinking   as I stared out
through thick glass   & a cheap red

 I was deaf   all was bleary   airless

this is Bottom   I thought   but was wrong
 I was wearing the hole in Bottom

the bottle still had it over me
 I was its tongue

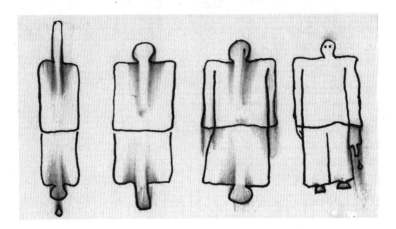

8

Novelty Shop

Hey kids   read this book
How To Improve Your Sex Life

a padded box   like a *Reader's Digest* anthology

when opened   it holds a strapped-in flask
& two tin shot-glasses

.

This dribble-glass   has a floral design   cut into it
the central vein   of each leaf   a hidden slit

drink here   to let leak   a joke-fire   harbinger
toy slobber

.

When I lift this little coffin's lid

a plastic skeleton rises   & pees   gin
in an arc   while a tune plays

get your mouths ready

.

Look how the pepper shaker's wee pole
fits into the salt shaker's wee hole

.

I'll buy your warts   if you pull my finger

9

After the party   a body no one knows   passed-out
down between coat-bed   & wall

then   like a square-dance caller   the host's refrain

Time to go   Bub   come on   (laughing)   *come on   hey
wake up   hey   it's time to get going   come on*

•

Don't talk to me about gyres

coning is when a wet brain hemorrhages

& slips through the base of the skull
down the spinal column

don't talk to me about *Vortex*

10

I will not wear the mask of either parent
will not be demoralized or enraged

won't stare at the floor & have no voice
nor grit my teeth to block my voice

I will not fill a room with smoke
or a trunk with bootleg

will not talk to pets like people
& then shoot them

you've read too much
there's something fierce to say

without a mask I am no past
without a past I am an amalgam devoid of loyalty

except to the presenting moment
its deep accordion sigh

the next word has
my true ancestors within it

II

   Many chase it   apart here   rocking   a thumb out

binge or maintenance   suicide corteges

 a few emerge certifiable   small tune circuses

or they keep taking new hostages   or are taken hostage
déjà rage

many drift in & out   dangerous babies   whining for years
 & never touch a Bottom that holds

unarrivals   *indestitutions*   *erasions*

·

 Invited to speak   un-knot   the yelling   jumble

a lobo   a blamer   *non tremens mentis*   joins chorus

one beaded moccasin sings with you

12

   Fold chairs   make coffee   serve soup

pray when you don't know how to pray
 wait when you've never gotten anything by waiting
listen when no one ever listened to poor you

 make up some gods   even out of hatred & hunger
out of alley kindnesses & anagrams

 almost miss grace   as grace *verbs* its way through you
be graceful in sobriety unto others

 embarrassing as it is to think like this out loud

as risky as it is to write not Art but hard lessons
 or rely on little self-help slogans

Think Think Think   that's so stupid

 but when we were geniuses   we drank

13

  Many claim grace
& capitalize it

they find inchoate rescue   in the secret

>   *Can there dare be any secret now*
>   whispers the beaded moccasin

>   *Can there dare be any dogma now*
>   warns the talking fish

the big secret   that Grace is a verb

>   *Oh bullshit!*
>   rises the skeleton (Mr Bones)

14

  This is what I love
about the world   sometimes

 & am not afraid to say so
this morning

 here's me   allergic to everything
especially horses   dogs   cats

 my pet peeve   smoking

& here's my beautiful daughter   in Costa Rica
 rescuer of cats & dogs

here's me   Virgo   rash   mouse   puppet

 put a Dr Johnson wig on it   make it laugh & dance
albeit sober   the whole blathering chit

 & here's my son   I haven't talked to in ages
he's so much like my dad

 who would say nothing   then say   *Now you understand*

but wait   here's my dad   & my son
 having a smoke   & a drink   together   on horseback

 soon   I'll have them dismount

 soon   they'll be kicking the daylights   out of some asshole
who looks like Phil Hall the poet

 these *living* daylights

 I sing

15

    The linked haiku

        nick-name / back alley / postal code

of all our old addresses

      ·

    After watching Mike Leigh's film   *Naked*

for the 8th unemployed time   house-sitting   here   we sang
bankers   in bunkers   go bonkers

in that house   near 41st & Fraser   until Russians bought it
all one winter our crack-up line was   *methane w/ rabies*

above this laundromat   preserves glowing   in siege
we called ourselves   secretly   *The Mary Pratt Vowels*

then we were sleeping inside   an orange parachute   on the 3rd floor
of that empty   rank   Chinese warehouse   above Water St

      ·

    A scent link

        ni k na e / ba k al e / po al c de

a blind mail-out

16

Dichten = Condensare

Basil Bunting's   then Ezra Pound's   equation

to canto   is to densify   besiege   ensnare

No   says Bottom   *to canto   is to loosen*   add   gather   over-say

Waitmake = Foliate

.

Slobber → sobber → sober

.

Delirium   is   to go off the furrow

& furrow is   cut   cult   cunt   culture

so to leave *Delirium*   is a re-entry   of culture

line   row   digit-count   cuneiform   Olson's *polis*

admit all   beseed   cornucope   embell

.

Sober is a matriarchy

17

Wish 1   safety   not security

lockless   doorless   roofless   nameless

each bead   its tiny hole   a note
strophes   the ramparts   of its formlines

now I am out here   with no lurch key

just my skeleton   working on its welcome

·

Wish 2   inch transformation   not magic

when   if   could   might

barley casserole   Scrabble   a geranium

my pulse   cack-cack

extravaganza   enough

·

Wish 3   archival improv

collage / montage   water / flour / newsprint

of codicils   & sacrosanctities   make a paste

will my new face   construed
from a pulp   *a past*   of facts   be a mask

no   the old facts   worshipped
vehement Chronos   were the mask

better   this raw documentary farce

these grimacing syllables

18

Recovery   may be   uncovery

but health   is not   who did what to whom

our drunkalogs   are court documents
of the good stories   that un-tongued us

·

Keep finding   a rage-line   or a joy-line

so ornery   surrounded by lies   & complex

·

Each day   I obfuscate   down to
& stay with   my rage   or joy

as Bottom   ferries me   in all my ambivalence
toward   not truth   but pattern

·

Only language

its etymology   limestoned as sound

lace   not *place*

holds me together

19

Deterioration sings without desire

our well-water is hard & turns to lime

 it ruins our water glasses by a milky crust

what we flush turns to sand & brambles

 down from the birch knoll   those are the weeping beds

& a doe eating blackberries

 deterioration sings without design

20

That hum   is Hum   at the feeder

the news from Tunis   probably

then again   she sips   at the feeder   & is gone
as I take note

by gap   & hum

.

A toy compass   *still quivering*   I found   along the road

fits perfectly   into   from a drawer   a Diamond   bottle-cap   (Guyana)

here   /   I have compounded   another thingamajig   for you

made two odd things   less simple   further odd

not one amen   or connivance   depends on this   offering

it has no need   no name   no need of a name

21

  I wipe my glasses   the better to see Hum
drink sugar-water

  swipe the mirror   to see myself   stupefy back

am again changed into   what I am called to

  this fraying   hay-twine   tinsel-smithy   & crimp-rust
alphabet

  a ph bet

by which Bottom   swears off   aim
  to invent directions

22

 Our kettle
sat full of vinegar all night

 to cut the lime build-up

this morning I forgot   & plugged it in
& made coffee

pickled sludge

 what an idiot I am
to seek the wild mirror lyric at 62

 through sour sand & lime

besmirched trills

2014-2020

Dot & Cec

To shut up
used to mean   hide well   scrunch / wait

now it means   I'd lose them

·

I may speak ill
of my parents   but who would hear of them

else by this plaint

·

Me telling on them   of them
is now their only   dilapidating   constitutor

this engraved   no

Screen & Costume

They never found me
when they found me   that cold morning

*Dobbie   was standing in the stall   sucking his thumb
sharing his quilt   with the logging horse   Blackie*

I had found my quilt   they had taken it   away from me
& hidden it   on Blackie

it was not my quilt   anymore

a self   is not a self   it is a screen   to get through
away from   who you would have   had to   have been

a slap   my wet thumb   drying   in the cold air

let out   Blackie rolled   in the new snow   in the barnyard
I didn't see how   she would ever be able   to get back up

her shitty   wet fetlocks   were flying

·

In breath   *this costume*

I have achieved   everything   I wanted to   I am real
when young   I never could have said   *I am real*

showing off   & mouthing off   were crimes

I had speaking parts   that were hiding places   where *real* meant   both
full of one's self   & empty   lost   in a book   or test

by these little words   my coat of many colours   this poor theatre

low   & beholden   I am real
but even now   the risk   a backhand   out of the air

for putting on   the air

Dream Babies

I am pulling   my glove on   with my teeth

a black hand   is coming out   of my mouth

the shadow-turkey   in everything   I say

·

The English Department   Men's

in the stall   nowhere   to put the bunch of keys
I'm carrying   so after I sit down

I drop my keys   into the empty   crotch of my pants

then I forget   stand up   pull my pants up   & feel the cold keys against my

a slight jangle   oh scoop them out   fast

·

Our boys & girls   in the Service   are dreaming   of sticks
their great-grandfathers   when young   pretended   were guns

the Dream   the Mission   & the Game   are now equal

*find & burn all of the stick-guns your grandfathers played with
ensure   in this way   that your real guns   never sleep*

Across the river   that is 16 years   of psychiatric talk
I see my dead parents   who are now   my oldest children

the river I used to be a fish in   a river they were land under

they don't recognize me   I pretend not to   recognize them
the woman says   Look at that old guy   across there

the man says   Maybe he can spare   a smoke

I don't smoke   never have   they know that   or should
besides   we are too far   apart now   to throw a smoke

maybe it's not them   /   talked out   I wave   & head inland

 ·

A light on a podium   & an audience I can't see   always listening

their silence   beseeches   my inadequacy   for a pure note

unfound   *then found*   then   unfound

behind me   on the dark stage   a darker shape

a Baby Grand   its tank-monstrance   the canon

Abuse

There is a praxis-delight   even in the shame
of returning   again & again   to this unerasable   subject

my subject   at last   slowly revealing itself   one I share with many
who are silent   but no less busy   at the forge
that still wants to be   way too late   an unfound motherlode

I tinker   toward inexhaustible   exfoliation
a surrendering defiance   dovetailed   toward ultimacy
these deformed   ignored   bristle-truths   cornered   smooth   to a hum
I also risk   gauche bluntness   while repeating myself
into patterns   that surprise   & help

random is a kingdom too   its fiefdoms confederated by collage
invite everything in   but not anything
the poem doesn't want a subject   it wants visionary accuracy
though only by long topic-digs   will the ugly truths
relax   into inarticulate   generosity

I envy my colleagues   who have no shame
but pity those   who are all facility   no compulsion
it doesn't have to be a trauma   let it be the tiniest preoccupied quirk
if we haven't found our zone-focus   we must scavenge
many subjects   flaunting borrowed opinion   or authority by degree

hungry for delight   & sincerity
but desperate   for a subterfuge   traditional-yet-hip
we write a precocious tone-confusion

we abuse design   by imposing knowledge   on music
& the rage-line   or the joy-line   eludes us

Drugs

Wiped   on acid   at Paul Diamond's cottage

the Mothers of Invention   squealing   I opened the Bible
  to Jesus's face   & watched it change   rapid-fire   into every face

that has ever existed   then at dawn   we started the bulldozer
  & drove down Main Street   like hockey stars
another night   *Blue Double-Dome*   in Fenelon Falls   near the locks

 I turned into a sea turtle   it crawled   through wet gravel
one of my flippers   nudged   Mom's skull
  Doug Moran's dad   Dr Moran   who could drive with his belly

while rolling a smoke   was drunk   on his snowmobile
  when he went through the ice   at Christmas   on Pigeon Lake
so Doug stole cases   of codeine cough syrup   we drank

3 bottles at a time   with tubes of *Gravol*   laughing   blind
at high school   up the back stairs   on all fours   our lips purple
  but that next July   needles   & speed   came to town

to cottage country   the loud   visible   air shook   its jungle
  pop-can-tabs   in me   I couldn't stop   yapping   for days

jittery   terrified   ruthless   my spiritual life   *zilch*

A Fontainebleau Dream Machine

You say   the Art Gallery   in Windsor   is gone

from along the river   Casino Corp bought it   tore it down
& put the art   in a warehouse   *somewhere...*

when D'Arcy   was a toddler   learning to walk   in 1978
his mom & I   still graduate students   *hillbillies in the big city*
was my joke   we would take him there   on Sundays

& let him run   & fall   in the clean   open rooms
his mom volunteered   as a docent that year   she met Roy Kiyooka
whose *Fontainebleau Dream Machine*   collages   scared me

but there was a sculpture   of a pioneer family   as if thrown out
on the open balcony   where people went   to smoke   figures posed
of rough wood   mere fence rails   expressionistic   in the weather

in my head   each time we went there   to try to be a family
I made up a little story   about how that balcony   was a visit home
I wrote a stupid poem   called *Pioneer Sculpture*   it said

this assemblage   *was* my family   slapdash   a joke   wet   rotted
the empty tankers   churning silently by   the Gallery windows   all day
like clouds   were the plowshares   I used to find   in the stone-piles

in the ice   grinding & cursing   as it broke up   the river   I heard
my dogs   long dead   shot   ripping a groundhog apart   between them
as if they somehow knew   & were acting out   again   the real story

there is no heritage   for Crazy   or Outlandish
Desperate is always on its own   then everyone pays   & stands in line
to get in to see   how all that audaciousness   is owned

I'm not so crazy anymore   D'Arcy is almost 40   his mom's in Texas
Roy Kiyooka is dead   I cherish now   how Roy improvises
lost gloves   his old mother's talk   hot air balloons   & pears

I am not afraid   as each day   writing a poem   A to Z   *upper limit*
lower limit   I drag that rough   pioneer sculpture   into the canon
of the dark warehouse   & dump it right beside   all the other Art

each morning   my family   folk art   has dragged itself   back outside
rotting in the weather   is part of its savvy   I have to learn   to let it

I have to learn   how to turn my illegitimacy   into Fire & Form

Ars Poetica

Speak   O Toothless One
my dad used to say   if we made a rude noise

we'd wave our hands   & grin   but I'd cringe too

because my own   O Toothless One
had already been   *compromised   breached*   by my cousin Clint

inside my secret   I was ashamed   to have a body
ashamed to speak   of it   crudely   or lightly

I feared   this I am   had no song   except fear

later   when I read in Von Franz   how the folk-cunt has teeth
I wished my ass had had teeth

there is   no other way   than bluntly   to say this   without lying

or betraying   the lyric   mammal courage   that is real music

in our miraculous   disavowed   routine   working systems
I cannot hear plain old animal husbandry   or joy in its stall boots

as I was meant to   I am squeamish

I dare not smear with wit   or cheapen with harmony
this widest possible song's   onslaught-rescue

I work toward an intimacy   an intricacy   approaching absurdity
spielraum

from eked notes   of self-loathing   & affinity
I invite a discordance

that cherishes   & defies

Distance Is Health

May my three sisters   I never see any more   outlive me

as the stats predict they will   though two of them are older
   & may my partially deaf   estranged son   know only health

though he drinks   & smokes in anger   like his grandfather did

for I am happy   & safe at last   in my disowning of them all   *safe*
   & happy-as-I-can-be   tinkering away   stretching this tiny focus

but if they get sick   & die before me   I'll have to go to their funerals

I'll have to see them again   or almost   in coffins   or fires
   I'll have to bow my head   as if there were a prayer in me   for them

Jehovah's Witnesses   abortion clinic picketers   haters of gays

I'll have to face their families   that I gladly know so little of
my own health having come slowly   by distance   & selfishness

my fear is that   if my scarred relation to them   is exposed   again

I will rot quickly & die   as if a curse were reopened   or hang myself
   in a relapse panic   as I used to fear I would do   when I still drove home

if I had to   maybe if I am far enough away   I won't be expected

to show up   why would I have to   even if I lived in the same township
I hate what ties me   like a helpless child   to what almost killed me

they will never admit that sexual abuse & drunken neglect really happened

I hate the religious ad campaigns for Parenthood as sacred   even when
   the child   hammered   attacks with cut up photographs   as hard evidence

I hate the precious   vague   spiritual optimism   of an easy lyric   too

(like newsletters   from Health Food chains   offering zany recipes)
we survivors prefer   as in Raymond Carver   to serve it cranky

I have sought wider   less bitter ways   to hold language   but it cramps

I tried to write like Bill Stafford   everything gets a voice   *hard for us all*
but found this miserable rant voice instead   honesty's long squeak

so I wish those strangers   from the same foul nest   well   I do

but I hope to die first   in Dublin   or Lisbon   with many books
open   nervously content   grateful for no news   from home

though I expect   I'll be let know of their passings   then I'll attempt grief

& attack myself   a bit   for my hard-heartedness
I cannot forgive myself   for loving them ruthlessly still

despite how they betrayed me   & cursed me   & turned me away

as I betrayed them   & cursed them   & turned them away
in their bewildered love of me   they had to be equally ruthless

may they thrive   & thrive   until I no longer thrive

Joe Junkin

I am sick of keeping up a quaint pretense
of language optimism   or some sloppy nod to the experimental

the legendary Joe Junkin   who came to school on skis all winter
& was later the goalie for the Bobcaygeon Ti-Cats
when they won All-Ontario   & took the fire truck out
waking the whole town up

taught me to tie my laces   in grade one   at Red Rock School

when I put my foot up on the rim of the bathtub   & stare at my laces
& can't remember how to tie them   for a moment   at 62
remembering Joe   & that fire-siren   the story of it

I am thinking about the form   that is a bow

soon I'll call my slippers   //   my blades

I wanted words to come at me   like pucks against my mask
but have wasted my life writing neat   tight designs

trying to tie it all together
with metaphor   such pretentious crap

as I come to the Boy's Exit   & can see the frozen pond
I face this stupid-hearted disappointment

there is nothing to stop its whisper with   but assemblage

& this old compulsion   not to be silent

Aubade

Glum in town at 12 I saw
each church-goer as one fuck

proof of abuse's whisper

you can't see it   but everyone
 & everything alive   is going at it

I didn't want to grow up to be the abuser
 who by violence to others makes himself unafraid & alone

I didn't want to be overwhelmed & crazy either

in my pew I made up a rude song

I wasn't touched enough properly
 as if to be taught the alphabet of skin

the flaw drawn here feels weak & shameful

but the poem is less of a victim by its telling

it is May in our woodlot   I am 62
 the new leaves   lit   are parsing   as they maw

bifurcation   invites into even me   the sacred

Failure

I should print out my new book
scatter its pages in the maple bush   & let it go at that

but I won't   I'll publish it   if I can

I'll proliferate   by articulate stratagems   the pretense
of sniff & growl

．

It will be   as if another   useless   19th C armoire
had been carpentered   from this phantasmagoria

called identity   panic   articulation

my book   will be a creature's denial   of crookedness
though it parade   as a celebration   of crookedness

living in Mondrian   I would Pollock

．

A Whitman line   is a breathless parcel

one long out-fling   folded & creased
again & over   in-on-itself

gagged   where the Heidelberg   pounds   its rhetoric

in all directions   on schedule
to outbid   the citizen's erratic pulse

arrives geometric clout

orderliness in type-drawers   *yesterfang*

any swirl   any Woodstock   must submit to
margins

& the cast iron   oil-smelling   cut

．

    Even to use a printer   to copy pages
  for scattering   in the wet bush

  would be a concession to geometry   over windfalls

  Flaubert's costume   Craft
   is technology's costume   Folio

  but where geometry fails   *scribble here*

   we might still find   oval aberrations

  & an uncaulked   illiterate horizon

   its pulse

．

  The actual sap   not syrup   is clear yet sodden

  it tastes of an ancient   cold   language   pre-process
   my poems   bow & scrape   for lack of

  pretend to know   but can't

  that unboiled calligraphy   I keep trying for
  is only a folk tale   about a claw-hold

A New Book

I said too much   too proudly   too soon

the imitative   had not burned down enough

to be silent was what felt reckless then

·

I tried to articulate   what would be praised

awaiting torture   I bite my tongue
I taste my silence pressure

·

The silence I knew   was a township   larger than a globe

I got out of there   to go on about   The Silent Township

·

I included words   so silence   had form
now silence   is *from*

·

You do not understand

I was not trying to be a somebody

I was trying to not be nothing

Design

Mornings   I see how a poem

in its winking bid   for specialness

is an avoidance performance

ashes   from the coal-shuttle   thrown

ash-dust   lofting   to the trees

smoke-like   but room temp   un-among

unmoved   as it maneuvers

to say my one line / to say my one line

I have whittled a little effigy flute

my handwork   a desperation-focus

a bare-assed run across an open field

shame   athwart   whitening   furrows

a magpie   shouts *Fox*   with a twang

as it hops   clearly a man   across the stage

those who study fox & magpie designs

will find no blood   or message   *In conclusion*

a poor theatre went this way

the poem as cowardice-doily

The design of a poem
> constantly
>
> under reconstruction,
>
> changing, pusht forward;

alternations of sound, sensations;
> the mind dance

wherein thot shows its pattern :
> a proposition
>
> in movement.
>
> The design

not in the sense of a treachery or
> deception

but of a conception betrayd,
> without a plan,
>
> completed

in the all over thing heard;
> a hidden thing

reveald in its pulse and
> durations;
> a fire.

                       Robert Duncan

VI

The Prodigal

1   *Guyana*

My poems circle failure   & abuse
these hot winter months

I mull what *subject* means   if this place is not my subject
or what *not-about* can mean

while slowly giving in to   unanticipated   *under-subjects*
my poems resist   being *of*   anything non-visceral

if they brandish the Occasional as subject   they are liars   cowards

but a grating   between *under-subjects*   & the *not-about*
invites arduous music   I admit to

a disbelief in progress   a worship of Anonymous
a pleasure only in revision   & a respect for awardlessness

my poems accept failure   as their only health or honesty

they know how *finished*   becomes *finessed*
how *making*   becomes *to market*

instead my poems turn doubt-mouthed   the lines I flaunted
are cheap or silly

I am often left with only one slap-welded combination word
or a few almost-destroyed stanzas

an unfittable   gnarled   not-me piece   *of what*

an unassociative   detritus-squeal
is all that's left   of so much   arrogant scrawl

ashamed of dexterity & articulation
ashamed to envy Larry Eigner his one usable index finger

I shudder at poems that are what I call   *typey-typey*
  in love with cheap play   they flaunt ego-blab

silence settles as an ash   blurring & isolating   each letter

I understand why people cut themselves

to narrow the palette

      •

The rainy season has come early

it cuts the wounded from the Visa Renewal line-ups

it pimples the open sewers fished from by white egrets

Ali   our landlord   who is a rice farmer
  has had his harvest delayed

he comes to our door at noon   bare-chested   with a gift of chickpea rotis
  called Doubles

Ann's bird racers were rained out again Sunday morning

  we call them hers   *ya call them hers we*

each cage with its own song-judge

      •

Here's a photo of us   huddled under our umbrella
out front   by   *The American International School of Peace*

a dilapidated   empty   incoherent   sputtering joke

we are on our way to Survival   for soda water & peanut butter

if you can see   it is our Canadian Tire umbrella

·

In the National Park   there is a creature   like you have never seen

it is very old   very strange   very beautiful   & shy
when it surfaces   you will not believe   how big it is   or how sad

it knows nothing about *National*   & has heard none of the bad news
about oil

rip out some long grass   at pondside   shake it in the water   & wait

those ripples   are it   swimming nearer   under the sound of your hand
get ready   to let go of   what it reminds you of

offer   *whatever it is*   your torn wayward bit   of all this

·

Downtown   by the National Library
the kiosk vendors   still yell at each other   about mosquito netting

though there are even fewer tourists than usual

Nobody goes to Guyana   Adrian   at The Word   had said

tied shut in big knots   the netting hangs   as bed-sets
from dripping Demerara trees   along KFC-strewn boulevards

I call them Demerara trees   not remembering the name I was told

to sleep   we crawl under   re-tuck   & are bivouacked   by gauze

unbitten in sleep   to become something else   flimsy
blue   pink   white   orange   mauve

each tiny mesh-gap   plugged bright   & swaying

a grey whisper   stampedes   all of our breathing-lights

·

*Not one blue saki   not one rice grain   not one kuras
not one blade of grass*

all Guyana   belongs to We   only in a song

Two days before we leave
up comes this loyalty to the place

a diluted snub   tasteless
The thing I will always remember about

I hate it here   & I hate Home   but I love being far away

every high adventure I have read   says   *dying in the colonies*
as marginalia   could outlast any main report

every plank   walked at sword point   by a minor character
has taunted me with silence

saying   *Go home   Little Visitor   & shut up*

book   your return   flight now
return your books   to the National Library

their sour   scored   between-the-war   pages
cheesing   to hornet-mash

•

This jungle rain   relentless   bored & sacrificial   overtakes
our canopy of rusted tin

we are stranded   between sleep's   semaphoring   snake-hair
& guttering patois

the crested   encrusted   forked   trill

of each drip-strand   each letter-bindle   rushed forward
as line-spatter

•

To never go home

to just-as-corrupt   just-as-sold-off   just-as-petty
but freezing   Canada

I have only to sleep   My Love

·

See   among spikes of glare   faith-goggled Miss Algernon

who for 6 months   has carefully date-stamped   each of our blue cards

& is now re-shelving   *The Fox in the Attic*   by Richard Hughes

inexplicably   a rich hunter   has found a dead girl
* & carries her small body home   in the morning drizzle   over his shoulder*

duty-exquisite Miss Algernon
  who loves her Saturday morning job   (I have loved seeing her every Saturday)

in this brown-glued   *Quinquireme of Nineveh*

 this galleon in framing-Vs   or at dry-dock   this white-basted library

its roof-struts   snapping   as full Noon shoves

yardarm swung-to   cracking of peg-joists

·

Even torn scraps of speech
force-fed   other scraps of speech   by ear   by hand

ayodeze   dog dog bark dog bark   rap-samba-blare

beneath this raging   foraging   hush

 become   overnight   deadly new   unforeseen creatures
syllable-chiggers

they hatch   in us   dash-barmed   shrill

II *Ontario*

I am never going home again

all of my poems start like this now

a dark moment opens   on a little pond in the woods
one duck huffs in   I hear its frantic reversals   settling

then a train monsters through   no lights on

•

When I looked inside the doll   through its leg-hole
I saw a rose-lit reverse-shape   a body-cave

just a kid   I held the little rubber leg in my hand   & looked in

I have sought that body-cave   in the eyes of wives
  girlfriends   women friends   women passing by

untrustworthy crotch   *Saturn* by Goya   I asked to be loved

I wanted to be hollowed out   & rose-lit
by association with women

because my cousin had torn my leg off
& violated my reverse-shape

because my mother had been emptied & couldn't see me
because my father hated me & was hungry

•

A slap in the mouth   I stopped singing

the period is my mandala

no   the sequence is my mandala

•

When I finally got away to university

my dad bought me a greatcoat
  from the Army Surplus   it was older than I was

& heavier   it wore me   in that legendary snowfall
  on guard   outside your dorm
in my Lennon glasses   they would call them now

 its brass buttons   had anchors on them
I traced with cold fingers   I had done up even the top one
  Dr Zhivago   *Sgt Pepper*

Dad got away   almost   just the once   by enlisting
  but never made it overseas   unless drunk in a park with a leg broken
in 7 places is overseas

 so of course when I was leaving home   what was left of it
he would buy me a greatcoat   & of course
 I would get sloppy drunk inside it   as if in a play

a snob about what I'd been reading
 I waited   outside in the snow   all night for you

whose name I forget now

•

When my ex-lovers close their eyes

I hope they can see the sacred animals
 I meant to paint inside them

that guy   oh he was like a shot dog
  had crawled into Chartres   to be healed

I can see the sacred animals
 they meant to paint inside me

.

Reading stopped the overwhelm

around the adventurous plot   past bathos
  through the littered woods

the dark branches inter-lap   & parlay
  by shadows   a disjunctive tapestry   shrug-loud

there are no field-recordings of this panic
  Artaud's catacomb noises on radio come closest

I have tried to write near the overwhelm

these poems have not been worth it

.

I have stood   the unexpected   clean weight
of shame   as it turns to defiance   then patience

there is in me now   a willingness   to stick around
as I balance   my wayward parts   at odd angles

I might soon forgive myself   as I rip my published books apart
to make new books   that don't kowtow   & aren't so bio-blinded

I am almost ready   to hold someone's hand   & watch them die
or let someone hold my hand   & watch me die

not someone   Ann

Ontario's aggregate hills are low
& uncomplaining in their grandeur

now the smell of water-mint   now the smell of jimsonweed
rises from looking that far

I ran away to join the circus
& found only a Pepsi truck   on its side in the ditch in the sun

dark hot glass bottles   shapely
in the grass   were strewn along both sides of the road

north   the Galway Road

free foreign medicine
& no way to uncap any of it   but violence

I'd like to say   I disavowed my inheritance   rage

logged swamps   sunken floating bridges
rusted wire   a hawthorn outgrew   to grip

but I poisoned myself   a sideshow   angrily   for years

I'd like to say   I turned off-map
 & found   in burnt quartz crevasses   blueberries

but the berries I ate   tasted of road-salt & paw
tasted of pissed-on crazy quilts

& those 19th C studio portraits
with their middle-parted oily hair   & fake Greek back-drops

too many exacerbated collusions   too many bony suckers

land fill   I spit Shield ink

my choice was   vanish (not far)   or varnish
 but to vanish   *applies* a varnish

now the smell of water-mint   now the smell of jimsonweed
rises from looking that far

I cherish   my earned balm   distance

I used to climb a cedar tree
& at the top   lean   with the tree
to reach the next tree   then see how far
across the cedar bush I could go
without coming down

no one ever came to find me

now all of my poems end like this

I get so sick of myself

that's what home is

VII

Pressure

  I am almost   as far away
  from Bobcaygeon   as I can get
   62   in Gravy   Kentucky
  untornup   on this bench

  that tree's a swamp cypress
  it stretches   its shadow's tip   this far
   each day   to this bench   & rests
  its wavering aim   here too   awhile

  something like belief
  has been putting pressure on my   *ohmygodula*
   everything is enhanced   distorted   my shadow seems
  to whisper   *the point is not the point*

  I rest on this moldy bench
  at the top of the cypress's shadow
   & watch the far end of my bench's shadow
  stretch its h   as far away

  as it can get

Mentored

   We won't learn much   from the little masters
  who invite us back   to our first skills

 refuse   hide   don't sleep   chant

as if to reinvent the alphabet   our needles sail
 we sew a Sampler

       •

We want to be inside their hands

right when they said to us   so oddly well
  these unexpected invitations   to trace

their choices   word & line   we fable back
  to what were   after all   accidents

       •

 When   to the Mardi Gras vulnerability   in first skills

ma ma   hold on   look-see   the quick fox

we return   the Unknown has been copied   & our own
pathetic unknowns   await us   like sheep

       •

There is no way home   from dexterity   says a dropped stitch

welcome to the pickled inaccuracy that is used metaphor

you have failed the Art of Failure test
& are qualified for perilous worship

Ashbery

He invented low surrealism

or found it   her   in the 50s   wandering the streets
of an Erie Canal barge town   lost

she was holding an egg-beater   & wearing a snood

now when there's company   & there's always company
at least she won't get all André Breton on us

& say   *Where's the egg-beater*

polite she is   & funny in a distracted
retrospective way   catty   my Lord   scathing even

but dissipated-scathing   you know

an American   after all   back from Paris
saga-voweled   piquant   bored

a looker away   out of windows   in mid-sentence

whatever is out there   she pretends not to notice

Oh yes   she was talking about Ashbery

Yawpless   *he substituted a laundromat-hum*
of rolling twaddle   *& eventually*   *it became prophetic*

who knew that's how we sounded

but that's how we sound

Tremulous

I used to hate my life   now I love it

I do   I realize   as Laura Smith is singing

then panic   *I wish I still hated everything
I wish I were locked shut*

I love Laura Smith's singing

though it hurts   like jumping off   when in her voice
our fossil highlanders
                              ignoring borders   & cursing first fences
go on night raids   again

with us   in us   *Come on!*
to defy the Closures   the Clearances

I smell smoke along the song-lines

we are not storage lockers   or gravel pits

we are first growth   & rock cliffs   tremulous
under water
                    the far low blue hills   teeming wide

or   more likely   we are the audacity it takes
to whisper such lies to ourselves

& believe them   or half believe them

while Laura Smith is singing
of how to fix her own gate
                              then leave it open

Oboe

Now all is forgiven
would someone please tell those Presbyterian hacks
in Canadian Studies
what Robert Duncan said
vowels the spirit / consonants the body

our gift was for small words without punctuation
we tried to be offhanded
about what was crucial
we could pry the lid off a nothing-phrase
& up would come the stink of America
a dry thirsty cough in church
some drifter who had slept in his car

when a priest rocks on your porch every Sunday
sipping whiskey with you near the bridge
it is easy to write good poems
but when the priest dies with nylons in his fist
it is easier to write fiction
there is more to describe than to sing of

pray again a vowel's lilt will usher in repetition
pray your body knocks again against its own silence

let's take off our heavy canvas sacks
of mail from the border wars
let's watch *Laura* together again
what a malicious dweeb Clifton Webb is

if we sit through the credits
the opening titles will roll again
& that sappy overture as it swells again
will be swell

Primitive

After horses   trees were our horses
they grew harness-collars   around holes
  where limbs had been cut   or had rotted off
thanks to bark beetles   *Curculionidae*

trees pulled   the long furrow
of the laid-open book   & of the part to the tresses
breath   it is all breath   down into us   & our lungs
fed leaves   the wild blue oats   of an exhale

trees stood   our lives-long   balancing
as they waited for   our gee or haw   all we had to do
was say Elm   Baobab   Hawthorn   everything
likes to hear its name   spoken   as a direction

but we thought trees   were wood   were stationary
now no trees   no air   only metaphoric air

      ·

It won't go the way you paid into or planned for
you can't have the procedural dignity you think is your due
  there will be mishaps   velvet bungles   a wrong entrance
no groundskeeper on Sunday   a slipped rope's whisper

what do you care anymore for vaudeville or decorum
done with all imagining   you are only a stage
  being taken apart   & packed away   with its gaudy costumes
these props   they always look so heavy   but never are

passive passive passive   sing the busy stage-hands   to & fro
they are insects now   but they used to be your relatives
I says the bark beetle   I rocked her cradle   till she fell asleep
I says the spider   no one was prouder of that kid than me

I says the worm   I will teach this fallen form   again
to spell   *worm*   backwards

My son D'Arcy is an artist   he draws zombies
one time he took me to an art show   by a friend of his
it was in a comic store   on display were SARS masks
each painted   Manga   Kabuki   Slasher

eventually   I got the drunken phone message
he thought I was shit   he was going to sue me   for writing
these little   ruthless   guilty poems   about him
no one reads   but me   q & him apparently

that was 10 years ago   I want to say
*he & I   must look almost the same now   immune
in our demon-masks   inherited muzzles*
but that's a bad poem right there   we always fail

if we get too smart with metaphor
we're better off drawing zombies

    ·

Not shy   not red   not rare   a robin
heralds   grey & green   shell & rain   egg & worm
its song   a brief soliloquy   variates   its verities
fly home   all ye   undiagnosed cancers   in Economy

to awake   in a B & B   at dawn
Grendel   naked   alone   & simply   listen
bleached sheets   white   crisp   bleached sheets
is almost   a breakthrough   into   holiness

but it is the *almost*   that carries   what primitive
wholeness   there can be   close to us   as hollowness
clean sheets   a cough next door   & robin song
here is early evidence   of a Merlin factor

by every hymn-list denied   though still at weave
in the middle-grounds   on our behalf

Carcass & Filo

Pessoa   on the 28E trolley   in a fog of bachelor tobacco

amid the crush & strap of bodies   is either becoming a Fascist
or he loves every rebarbative aperçu's funk & dither

more & more   each dull tea time

    ·

In my half-sleeping field mind   old potatoes   & a dead dog
trundled in burlap   are left out   to rot in burgundy thistles

    ·

Stalled in glare   at a yellow light   a migraine aura coming on

there's a tap at the car window   an old man hands me a flyer
Don't Feed the Coyotes

he reminds me of my dozy in-laws   or he looks like one of the men

I cared for as an orderly back in '77   but those men are all long-dead
all near death in me yet too

    ·

Or I half-see an 80s open-mic   where Rudy Pong   is reciting

Casey at the Bat   next up Gwen to yell her sonnet   *pubescent blue babies*
what a nut-bar   she too belongs at the carcass

    ·

My dream: a filo alphabet curtain   in many languages   hangs

between   Erin Mouré   laughing   on skis   in the mountains
or dancing   at 41st & Fraser   /   & Erín Moure

slopping raw lentils out   from bilge-water   in a friendly morgue

she is trying to save everyone   *These are the last citizens*   she says
& there's that grimace   I tolerate the world for

Here come all of us animals now   our nothing-navels lost in fur

Moses   Lily   Dr Poisson   Ernie Alden   Link   Mr Smiley   dredged up
we winced the immediate day

it beat down leakage   dash & respite   shredded facts   sloppy tries

*John Van Wagoner   Grattan Woodcock   Lloyd Kelly   Father Doyle   Irene
Hidden Bernice*   our deeds had no hands

no point or gradation   no design   did not flirt   we articulated

the foreigner   inside the sacred mother   & will never be forgiven
for this raw disowning clarity   that is panic assemblage

·

Out of selection comes painful cattle   says Stein

·

As long as I am reading   *The Arcade Project*   Walter Benjamin
wakes up   eager & confident   each morning

·

Still we are brother & sister to all minutiae

Undressed

This year's escape   is to the west coast

BC   Victoria   a sojourn alone   at Mile 0
the stink of the shore   & an empty fridge   like in '79

3 months   the pens I brought   are still writing
I'm surprised   they are cheap pens   grabbed in a hurry
I've only had to throw one out   Park Town Hotel

it's true I'm not using them obsessively   or maybe I am
what I write   in my Chinese notebook from John's Convenience
is mostly a record of the weather   *not so great*

I'm OK   sad   a friend back home is dying
I don't have many poems to show for my time here
though it seems an achievement   this morning

to trust enough ink is left   to take on the past tense
the pens I brought   suited me   & the journey
I had 3 sisters   was married 3 times

& had 3 children   seminal / aortal / connubial
was abused   had an early hernia operation
a late circumcision   the vasectomy

was in love 7 times   no   8
my violence / was silence   to disappear   I drank
bottomed   & reappeared   contrapuntal

I undressed my mouth
at the intersection of Niagara & Government

my insides are not where I'm from originally

K7H 3C7

My crunchy liver
my iffy heart   my legendary spleen
in the mornings   when it is still   at its darkest   I try to write
as I wait for the sun   or its grey semblance
   to lift   again   up over   dead birches   in the swamp

   or to infuse   an accurate   pervasive   un-curated   oddity
      everywhere   I have said all this before   *my lug nut pineal gland*
my groundhog stomach on the lawn   my deciduous kidneys
my pickled bagpipes   above the ancient freeway
these Miró devices   none of them mine   not really

   I like June better   as a month   for writing   about failure
those late   shaky   evenings   in mid-June
   the sun   setting behind Oliver's   near the point
will skim   the weedy bay   & haver   above Otty Lake
   to rattle   *the matchbox-holders   the stove-lifters*

the potato-mashers   the wire egg-baskets   the cant-hooks
   all nailed   to log walls   on the porch
a parody   of industriousness   that lake-light
   each evening   in June   it deliquesces   our forge
but it is November now   the days cough   abrupt   stringent

   a fire   I have constantly on   the wood is punky with mold
my poems are awful   in their fake vehemence
I am at work on that puppet play
   remember   we talked of writing one   for Xmas
   a spit & paste romp   as crude with flourishes   as incunabula

sick of being the dragon   sick of being the king
our hands emerge   shame-faced   abashed
naked puppets   hands   dappled by
   & also   hidden by   the history   they perform
Punch & Judy   give each other   the clap

A Great Beauty

I am not reconciled

as we become less apt
  like old words   bandied about
cheapened   misused

until there is no give to   no speaking well
those words   appropriated   by cheats   by high-hats
  words we once pegged out   wide   snug   & slept in   & made out in
our bivouac words   *solid*   *bogart*   *threads*   *drag*

now husks   laughed at   or fluffed   to mean
condo-lessness   *insurgents*   *disenfranchisement*   *reprioritization*
for shared mammal needs   such big words   leeched of history
& turned so bitterly against us

yet   despite everything   we still love our small   blunt   first words
they only look simple   but are perennial riddles   fingerings
we still find in words like   *union*   or *campesino*   the great beauty
& elegance   & defiance   they had

you will always be a great beauty to me
like the words   *rhubarb*   *defunct*   or *fuzz*   as we age
  & the rotten bastards   out to get us
become   also   our own bodies   itemized

to face   new attacks   from within
I will stand on one leg   & talk flap-doodle   into manifesto
I will see you   the way I've always seen you   as many
di mare   I will say each of our secret names

not as crumpled   discontinued   coinage
but like 60s lyrics   *take the load off Fanny*
we didn't really understand them   but we believed in them

obscurity   a blur of pride

NOTES

Local Produce

Written in first draft in 2015 during a 3-day experiment in outdoor writing—
"Framework"—at Fieldworks, a landscape gallery/site near Perth, Ontario

Other writers involved that first year were: Amanda West Lewis,
Amanda Jernigan, Michael Blouin, Matthew Holmes, Wayne Grady,
Merilyn Simonds, Christine Pountney, Jeff Warren, & Troy McClure

Paul Cezanne (1861-1906); Paul Celan (1920-1970)

The soldiers' names are taken from Homer's *Iliad* by way of Alice Oswald's *Memorial*, & from *In Parenthesis* by David Jones. *Hall Thurston* is a soldier's name from the war cenotaph in the park in Bobcaygeon

Charles Olson: "and Joe Blow got swap / up the side of the head" is from *Anecdotes of the Late War* (Jargon Broadside 1: Highlands, 1955)

Alfred Jarry (1873-1907); Robert Frost (1874-1963)

Alfred Jarry's play *Ubu Roi* notoriously initiated Modernism on December 10, 1896 in Paris at the Théâtre de L'Oeuvre—Yeats was in the audience

Robert Frost's poem "Stopping By Woods on a Snowy Evening" was published in 1923, between the wars, refuting Modernism

Massey-Harris (1891): at one time the largest agricultural equipment manufacturer in the British Empire

Massey: as in Vincent Massey, Governor General of Canada (1952-1959); as in Massey College & Massey Hall (Toronto); as in Raymond Massey (actor)

Harris: as in Lawren Harris, painter (Group of Seven), theosophist

This poem was published first in *Framework: Words on the Land 2015* (A Fieldworks Project), edited by Susan Osler, Sheila Macdonald & Chris Turnbull

Stan Dragland's *Wall*

A birthday present for Stan, December 2015

His sculpture / assemblage was exhibited as part of the show *Architec Tonic* at 2 Rooms Contemporary Art Projects in Duntara, Newfoundland from July 9th to August 28th 2016

Barthes, Roland. *Le Degré Zéro de L'Ecriture.* (Paris: Editions du Souel, 1953)

Binchy, Maeve. *Scarlet Feather.* (New York: Signet, 2000)

Johnson, Ronald. *ARK.* (Chicago: Flood Editions, 2013)

Royet-Journoud, Claude. *The notion of obstacle.* Translated by Keith Waldrop. (Vermont: AWEDE, 1985)

_____ *Objects Contain the Infinite*. Translated by Keith Waldrop. (Vermont: AWEDE, 1995)

Jackson Pollock, Joan Miró, Georges Braque, Geoffrey Chaucer, Mikhail Bakhtin, *Huckleberry Finn*, Joseph Cornell

Daphne Marlatt, Robert Kroetsch, James Reaney, bpNichol, Colleen Thibaudeau, Christopher Dewdney, Roy Kiyooka

Thanks to Peter Quartermain for the Kenneth Burke quote: a Keefer Street bookmark, December 20

An earlier version of this essay-poem was first published in *Notes on Assemblage* (JackPine Press, 2017)

Bottom

An early version of *Bottom* was printed as a chapbook of 40 copies for the HIJ Reading Series by Jay & Hazel Millar, September 2015

Nudie Cohn (1902-1984) was rhinestone suit maker to the country music stars

Other Bottoms: *A Midsummer Night's Dream*—Rimbaud's poem "Bottom"— Louis Zukofsky's study of Shakespeare, *Bottom* (1963)

The Mail from Tunis, probably—Emily Dickinson

condensary—that's Lorine Niedecker's word

Thanks to Patrick Lane, Fr Lawrence, Ali Blythe

Design

The Robert Duncan quote that shadows this poem is from *Derivations 1950-1956*. (London, Fulcrum Press, 1968)

Prodigal

"Not A Blade of Grass" is a song, almost a national anthem for Guyana, by Dave Martens

Richard Hughes. *The Fox in the Attic*. (London: Chatto & Windus, 1961)

"Quinquireme of Nineveh"—see "Cargoes" by John Masefield

Artaud—his censored radio play is titled "To Have Done with the Judgment of God"

Other Notes / & to Acknowledge

tatibitexto—stuttertext—a Haraldo de Campos word

"Typo" in an earlier version first appeared at Flat Singles Press

Niedecker, Lorine. *Paean to Place. Aug 1963.* (Kenosha, Wisconsin: Western Pattern and Light and Dust, 2003)

"Selim Sivad"—that's Miles Davis backwards: World Saxophone Orchestra, *Selim Sivad—a Tribute to Miles Davis.* Recorded March 2-3 1998.

"The Leap" was written in response & collaboration with Toronto artist Tim Deverell. An early version appeared in *Vallum / "The Leap" & "Falling" by James Dickey*

Montale's note to "Hitler Spring" (1939-46-56) reads: "Hitler and Mussolini in Florence. Gala evening at the Communal Theater. On the Arno, a snowfall of white butterflies."

Which may be translated as: *It & us—in in or in—at the un-at—on the no—a no—all of it—lies*

•

Early parts of "Translation," "Fireworks," "Dream Babies," "Carcass & Filo," and bits of other poems were written in response & collaboration with Ottawa artist Stuart Kinmond

Dolly Parton: "My Coat of Many Colours" / Laura Smith: "My Gate is Wide Open"

"Joe Junkin" stayed truer to its first principals thanks to a nudge from Liz Hay

"A Fontainebleau Dream Machine" was written for an international project to honour C D Wright, edited by Dong Li, spring 2016

"A New Book" appeared in *ARC*, but I've changed it since then, took out a part

Kiyooka, Roy. *the Fontainebleau Dream Machine: 18 Frames from A Book of Rhetoric* (Toronto: Coach House, 1977)

"Failure" has been printed on seed paper & planted along the Rideau Trail in 2020 as part of Chris Turnbull's *rout/e* project

"The Lyric" and "K7H 3M9" in earlier versions appeared in *CV2*. "The Lyric" also appeared in *Best Canadian Poetry 2018*

•

In Memoriam Laura Smith (1952-2020)

A longer husk of "Oboe" appeared first as "Eugene Mcnamara"—a broadside handout for a reading in Windsor, then in *The Windsor Review*, twice. This last form has evolved past homage, but Gene (1930-2016) was my teacher and friend, and one of my heroes

"Primitive" and "Undressed" appeared first in *The Cafe Review*—the Canadian issue

"Failure"—Illich, Ivan. *In the Vineyard of the Text—A Commentary on Hugh's Didascalicon* (Chicago: University of Chicago Press, 1993)

Marie-Louise Von Franz (1915-1998). *Animus and Anima in Fairy Tales*; *On Death and Dying*; *Time Rhythm and Repose*

•

Zukofsky—"The ungainliness of the creature needs stating"

Rukeyser—"Do I move toward form? Do I use all my fears?"

•

A few other parts of these poems were also published in *Notes on Assemblage* (JackPine Press, 2017)

or in *Alternative Girders* (above/ground press, 2018), or by Flat Singles Press on its website

But what does it matter where any poem or part or line appeared before? (Oh, "A New Book" appeared in *ARC*—which version?)

The parts shift & alter to find their best singing-proximities. Permissions and collage are at odds

I am grateful to Mark Goldstein, Erín Moure, John Steffler, Andrew Vaisius, Phyllis Webb, Meredith & Peter Quartermain

Thanks, Ann. Thanks, Brette. Thanks, Sam

Phil Hall won the 2011 Governor General's Literary Award for Poetry in English for *Killdeer—Essay-Poems*, which also won Ontario's Trillium Book Award, and an Alcuin Design Award. Hall has been nominated twice for the Griffin Poetry Prize. Pedlar Press has also published Hall's *The Little Seamstress* (2010). He has been writer-in-residence at The Pierre Berton House (Dawson City, Yukon), Queen's University, the University of Windsor, the University of Ottawa, and the University of New Brunswick. In 2012 he inaugurated a lecture series at Queen's University called *The Page Lectures*, in honour of Joanne Page. He lives near Perth, Ontario.